The Hidden Gems in Life

"Unlocking the Potential in Your Life"

Contents

Dedication…………………………………………………………..…Page 4

Introduction……………………………………...........…...………Page 5

What Are the Gems in Life………………………………..…Page 7

How to Become a Better You………………………………Page 9

Planning Your Future……………………………...............…Page 24

Your Goals……………………………….......…………........Page 31

The Book of Wisdom……………………………….......…...…Page 39

Good and Unhealthy Health Habits……………..……..…. Page 59

Let Us Talk About Money…………………………….…Page 66

Good Habits……………………………………………....…..Page 75

26 Hidden Gem ……………………………......………………Page 83

References and Citations………………………..……………Page 90

Dedication

First, I would like to give thanks to the almighty God for guiding me with wisdom and directing me to create this insightful book. To my mom, Janice Shaw who was always there to guide me in spirit and help me through the whole journey. I am doing this for her and my lovely daughter, Marlisa Shaw. I value my daughter as my strength. Indeed, you both have been my biggest inspiration. I would like to give a big thank you to my friend Kerdens Hall, without you, this book would have not been its best.

Introduction

Who would not want to discover the treasures hidden within themselves? The purpose of this book is to help you discover "**The Hidden Gems in Life**" that can change your life forever. The reader will gain wisdom, patience, gratitude, motivation, dedication, and much more. The most critical thing you will learn is how to become a better version of yourself. These mind-blowing tips and lessons can make your journey more convenient.

This page-turner book can indeed change you. You can see things differently when you have an insightful perspective. It will provide you with a whole new lens through which to view the world. Harkeem Shaw expertly writes this content. He could be considered to have authored this book as an essence of his life experiences. It focuses on self-help. As you read deeper into the book, you will notice certain changes in yourself. Eventually, you will be able to see a better you in the mirror. However, that is not all. It holds much more than your expectations. So, are you ready to jump in?

What are the Gems in Life

A "**Hidden Gem**" is something that is not well-known or popular but has something special or unique about it that inspires positive feelings. That is what this book is all about. I will show you many "**Hidden Gems**" to help you maneuver through life. This book talks about how to become a better person; it will teach you wisdom and how to plan your future and so much more.

In my many years of living and studying, I have discovered many Gems in life that I want to share with you. This book has many Gems you should treasure for the rest of your life. Some things you will agree with and some things you may not. That is okay, if you get something out of this book it will be well worth your time. **Time** is one of the Gems you will discover in this book, and it is the key element that makes everything possible. I am sure you will learn things you have never imagined before. So, sit back and enjoy **"The Hidden Gems in Life."**

This next section is all about **"How to Become a Better You**." It is full of wisdom and stoicism. Most of us are just mimicking mistake after mistake. This section will allow you to become a productive and initiative-taking person. "Let's begin."

How to Become a Better You

1.   **You are a special and unique person** and there is no one on this planet just like you. You were the strongest of millions of cells and you fought your first fight, and you won that battle and here you are, the only champion and the winner by a long shot. You may have heard someone say to you that they saw someone who looks just like you. The fact of the matter is that person reminds them of you. Trust me when I tell you, there is no one exactly like you.

2.   **Be thankful God made you** and never wish to be someone else; just become a better you.   If God wanted you to be someone else, he would have made you that way, so be unique, and be yourself. Love yourself, and take care of your mind and body, protect them both as it is

the only one you have. The mind and body are terrible things to waste. Remember, as a person thinks in his heart so is he.

3.   **I cannot tell you what to do**, but I can suggest to you what not to do. Do not sleep when you should be working. You will let precious hours slip away and poverty will hit you fast. Proverb 7:7 (Beware of becoming an "Empty Person—this is a person with no substance, no depth, no long-term visible growth, no discipline, working to buy shoes, to prowl the malls, to play video games, to waste their lives doing nothing of substance or worth).

4.   **Do not watch TV or play computer** games for one month and learn about who you are. You will be amazed at how much time you waste on games and television while denying who you truly are and knowing your full capabilities in this vast universe. You do not have time to waste, stop wasting time and get on with living an exciting and productive life.

5.   **Remember you must love yourself** before you can love someone else. Always seek knowledge of self, health, and wealth. Do not be selfish, be humble. Do not be religious, be spiritual.

6.   **What I found out in my studying** about what leads to a fulfilling life. I concluded that many religions discuss love as the key to a good life. Love is the key to peace and happiness.

7.   **You will attract the things that you ask for in life**, so make sure you know all the details. This is especially important. Create a vision board and see into your future, putting everything you want on it, and do not leave out any details. Plan for the best and put God to the test.

8.   **Take an aptitude test or job placement test**. Why, because it will save you time, money, and headaches; it will point you in the right direction at an early age. This has helped me tremendously in finding what I will like and what I will be good at in life. It is necessary to prevent you from stumbling from job to job. Find something that you love to do, and you will never have to work a day in your life. For example, people who love playing basketball are doing something that they love to do.

9.   **Finish high school.** Why, in this book I talk about how it is easier to keep up rather than trying to catch up. In high school, you should be with people that are going to college. Going to college is fun, you will learn a skill and meet different people from all social classes with which

you can grow. It will become part of your network when you graduate, some of your peers will further their education and go for their master's degree, MD, and PhD. These are the people you want to stay connected with. You want to surround yourself with people that are smarter than you. They say, if you are in a room and you are the smartest in the room, then you are in the wrong room.

10.   **Watch "The Secret**." This is one of the foundations to becoming successful in life. You must believe in yourself before you can believe in others. "**The Secret**" is all about "**The Laws of Attraction**." You must attract things that you want in life by believing in them and acting as though you have them already. This movie is a must-watch; without this movie, you might stumble and give up on your dreams.

11.   **Create a vision board**. You need a vision board to see where you want to go in life, and you need to see the things you want to accomplish in life. This **Vision Board** is also important. You must not only

think about it, but you must also see it and feel it, to make it happen in your life. With the vision board, you can experience the magic of thinking and seeing your goals right now.

12.   **Have a list of 25 things to accomplish** in the next 5 years. Why, your life should always be about accomplishing things in life. If you do not do these things, you are wasting your time doing senseless things that do not amount to anything in your life in the end. Now when you get older you will look back and say what did I do with my time, I accomplished nothing worth valuing or cherishing for my family. It seems like all I did was just go to and from work for 40 years. I went on vacation every year and I had fun, but in the end, which is all I did. Now, I can collect social security and maybe a pension. If that is all you want in life, go for it. What if you had planned to acquire personal goals in those last 40 years? Do you think you could have had a better life to leave behind for your family? Where is the rainbow at the end, what did I really accomplish? Do I have 4 streams of income coming from sources that I do not have to work at? Now my family must work for someone else, just like I did for 40 years. Something must change, and you must be the change to make things better for you and your family.

Write down 25 things to accomplish in the next 5 years and work on it and your life will be exciting and interesting.

1.
2.
3.
4.
5.
6.
7.
8.
9.
10.
11.
12.
13.
14.
15.
16.
17.

18.	
19.	
20.	
21.	
22.	
23.	
24.	
25.	

13.   **Record your daily life lessons** so you can remember them in the future and place them in a book so your family can learn from them. Carry a notepad and record your notes for the day. Write down what you learn during the day and keep a journal. It is especially important to write your thoughts down so that you do not forget them. Review your notes weekly and monthly so that you can keep the lessons fresh in your mind; if you do not do this you will surely forget them.

14.   **Albert Einstein said**, "An unexamined life is not worth living." Create your wisdom book, and pass it down to your family, so that they do not have to make the same mistakes. That is what I did for my family and yours.

15.   **You must remind yourself of** certain things to **do**. Read at least one lesson a day in this book, because we tend to forget the simple things in life. It takes less than a minute to read one lesson, so why not read a lesson and gain years and hours of knowledge and wisdom?

16.   **Remember most things are possible**, just put your mind to it. If you can conceive it, you can achieve it, all you need is a positive mental attitude. Do not let anyone stop you from your dreams or goals in life. Your goals are for you only and nobody else, only you can achieve your goals for yourself, and The Bible says, "Faith without work is dead." (James 2:14-22 ESV;NIV)

17.   **By understanding these lessons** in this book, you will save time, money, and maybe your life. Always pay attention when crossing the street, especially when you are with others and are on your cell phone. Please do not do that; people have become crippled by not paying

attention when they are crossing the street. If this book saves one person's life, then this book has done its job in helping someone.

18.   **Believe in yourself**, think positively, and always keep God in your heart. Your brain is capable of many things. You can be poor one day and think of an invention and become rich, it is up to you and the Creator. As a person thinks in his heart so is he.

19.   **Do not feed the fire** is all about arguing with someone about something that you believe is right. Arguing is a waste of time and energy and can cause a fight to break out over something very silly, such as if a chicken leg is white meat or dark meat. Just make your point and move on. Some people like to argue but remember you cannot argue by yourself.

20.   **Pay attention to your surroundings**. There are many messages all around you that God has planted for you to see, hear, and feel. We all have notions in our minds to do things and say things. Learn to listen to the universe, for it is always speaking to you. Here is a word of advice, if it is something you are supposed to do, just do it. You will be so surprised by the results. Learn to hear with your ears and see with your eyes and

feel with your heart. Trust me when I tell you, someone is always listening.

21.   **Always seek knowledge of self,** health, and wealth. Do not be selfish, be humble. Do not be religious, be spiritual. Do not rush into a business, always do your research first. Remember what Warren Buffett said, "Rule number 1, do not lose money. Rule number 2 do not forget Rule number 1.

22.   **Read, learn, and study what you want in life,** then write a 5-year plan and work toward it.

23.   **Love yourself** and take care of your mind and body; and protect them both.

24.   **Respect people** and their time. Do not take people for granted. Be true to yourself and others. Play hard, play fair, and play to win because the other man is playing to kick your butt. Life is one big game with some winners and many losers.

25.   **It is good to be a leader,** but also to know when to follow. A true leader knows when to follow, and your success as a leader is not only in

your ability to lead but also in guiding your team. Remember there is no "I" in **Team**. Think of a championship game and you are the captain; you can only win with good leadership and a good team.

26. **Think of the good times** in life, and do not forget the other times. Every day is an experience full of things to learn from, and this book is to help you keep track of your experiences. It is said that God will not bless you if your heart is full of hate and anguish. So, keep on thinking of the enjoyable times and your future ahead. Vision is one of the most powerful things to possess.

27. **Creativity is what sells** in personal behavior and business. Whenever you are selling something to someone, it must have a WOW factor to it. What is a WOW factor? You want your customer to say WOW that is nice when they see what you are presenting to them.

28. **Going to college**. If you cannot afford college, go to www.Udemy.com and they have hundreds of courses to learn from. The amazing thing about Udemy, most of their courses are around $15 to $20, you can also get a Certificate of Completion. This will level the playing field when you go out on your own and look for a career. You are not

looking for a job, you are looking for a career. Take an aptitude or career placement test to determine what career to go for, your results will show what you will be good at.

Only pick one of the first two results from the test, and you will be happy with what you do. This will guide you along your journey in seeking a career that you will love to work in. It worked for me.

29.   **Write down all your ideas** and inventions and pick one to make you money. They say we all have one innovative idea in our lifetime. Remember to do your homework first. **1**. Check online to see if it exists and do a self-patent search, this just requires your time. Go to www.Youtube.com and look up how to do a patent search. **2**. Ask your family and friends if it is a clever idea, and do not think they will steal your idea. Before you tell anyone make sure you have written it down and have two people see and understand it and sign it. You can also have them sign a **Non-Disclosure Agreement** letter also known as an **NDA**; if needed, go online, and see how to create one. Now create a **Provisional Patent Application (PPA)** and file it yourself. The cost at the time of drafting this book is about **$75.** The provisional patent application can include a hand sketch of the invention, so now you can show it to others.

This will give you perceived ownership for one year, giving you time to prepare for a utility patent. You can also contact me—the Author of this book—and I will be glad to help you. As an inventor myself there are many things to know before pursuing your idea. Such as, you want to make a few improvements to your idea, before filing a PPA (Provisional Patent Application). To learn more about inventing go to my other book called "**The Inventors Manual: Learn How to Invent Right**," By Harkeem Shaw.

30. **Never talk badly about someone** and do not prejudge anyone. Life is a circle, what goes around comes around. If you are talking badly about someone, trust me, someone is also talking badly about you. So, if you do not have anything good to say about someone, do not say anything at all about that person. Every time you open your mouth, people can see into your character and have an idea of who you are.

31. **Always try to tell the truth**. The truth builds good character, and it keep you honest. Lying always follows more lies. People hate liars and thieves. Do you want to be known as a liar or someone with integrity and honesty? This is your life to live, so make it truthful.

32.   **Love always** and be happy. You should treasure being in love, and it is wonderful being love.

33.   **Read self-help books**, go to www.YouTube.com, and listen to motivational speakers like Les Brown, Zig Ziglar, Jim Rohn, Earl Shoaff, Earl Nightingale, and Jordan Peterson just to name a few! They will motivate you to do better in life!

34.   **Always re-read these messages** in this book. This book is to not only help me remember, but it is for you as well.

35.   **Create your vision board**. Get a large card stock paper, about 24" by 36" and cut out or print some things you plan to acquire in life in the next 5 years. Examples would be a lovely home, a nice car, a partner that loves you, a successful business, money in the bank, good health, and living your dream life. This vision board you must watch day and night. Now here is the secret, you must act as though you have these things already and they will come to you.   Watch the movie called "**The Secret**." You will get a better idea once you see the movie.

36. **Make a 1, 3, and 5-year plan** and work on it every day and you will be amazed at how things just seem to fall into place. Now it is time to go to work! Do these things before going to the next chapter!

HERE ARE YOUR FIRST 5 GEMS

1. Take an aptitude test or a job placement test, this will guide you on the right path right away, saving you time and eliminating the guesswork.

2. Work on finishing high school, and college. If you cannot afford college, go to www.Udemy.com, and get certified in a field you love to do.

3. "Watch "The Secret." this is especially important and will guide you along the way.

4. Create a vision board, so you can see where you are going.

5. Have a list of 25 things to accomplish in the next 5 years and focus on its night and day.

Remember, this is not a sprint,

it is a marathon.

Follow these lessons and Gems and you will be on your way to a happier and more fulfilling life. If you have already completed high school and college, then you are off to a great start. The next thing you must do is watch **"The Secret**." Look for the one on YouTube that is **1 hour, 31 minutes, and 10 seconds** long. This is especially important to watch before moving on; if you skip this part, you might lose the understanding of the laws of attraction and how it works. Then after you watch "The Secret," take your time and create a vision board, then create a list of 25 things you will accomplish in the next 5 years. When you finish the 3rd, 4th and 5th Gem then you can go on to the next step. This should take you about 2 and half hours. This is the prep work, that you must do to be successful and to be a better you. Now you are ready for the next section called "**Planning Your Future.**"

Planning Your Future

Remember that a successful person is doing what they want to do in life! Did you know only about 14% of people are doing what they love to do, and the main reason is education? The rest are just followers, working because everyone else is working, not understanding their true purpose in life! Have a clear plan in life and follow your plans. I will guarantee that you will live a more productive life! Please do not just act, think.

37.   **We are control** through our subconscious mind by 95 percent and 5 percent by our conscious mind. The subconscious is program into us during the first 7 years of our life. Do you know what programs are you following?

38.   **Have 1, 3, and 5-year plans.** Why, if you do not plan your life someone will plan it for you. They will tell you what to do, when to take

a vacation, how many vacations you can take each year, how many sick days you can take, how much money you can make, and which holiday you can take off from work. They have your life all planned out for you; now would it be better if you were in control of all these things? Well, you would need a plan to make that happen. Create a plan on how you are going to accomplish your 25 things in 5 years and make sure you make these 25 things worth achieving.

39.   **Have a list of 10 things to do** weekly. Why, a list will guide you through your day, and this will bring you closer and closer to achieving everything on your list.

40.   **Grade yourself** in doing your 10 weekly things toward your goals. Why, the things that you have on your list you must take very seriously and do not play with this. This is your future and your goals to accomplish in the next five years. Create a monthly calendar and grade yourself weekly, and your goal is to get an "A" **score for 12 weeks**, then this will form a habit. **Accomplish 10 or 9 out of 10** and you get an "A" for the week, 8 or 7 out of 10 and you get a "C", and 6 or 5 and under you get a Big Fat "F" for the week. Use a calendar to measure your seriousness and accomplishments. Keep on trying until you get **12 "A's" straight** in a

one-year calendar. This will create a habit and a good one for achieving your goals.

41.   **Act as though** you have it already.   Why, this is also important; you must walk, talk and act as though you already have all these things on your list, and then this is where "**The Law of Attraction**" come in.   As you move in life the universe will bring these things to you. You must be in alignment with and vibrate on the same frequency that you are believing and acting on.

42.   **Always think positively**. Why, your attitude is a big part of getting what you want in life. You must always think positively in life and not negatively. You must show the world that you are a positive person, and the world will act positively around you. Is your glass half empty or half full? Whatever you decide you are right.

43.   **Mind your own business**; that is, every day you should be moving closer toward your goals in life. When making a mistake or what appears to be a mistake just learn from that experience and move on. Remember there are opportunities all around you! You just need to find the one that fits your life.

44.   **One of the most difficult things** is to find your true purpose in life! How do you go about finding it, or does it find you? Life is about finding your true purpose! Do you know your true purpose? If it came to you today, would you know it was here; would you feel it, see it, touch it, or just believe in it!?   Only you can tell what that is! Most of us travel our whole life not knowing our true purpose in life! Don't you be one of them; are you doing what you were born to do? The reason you cannot find it, you always had it. Now it is time to reveal it.

45.   **Study yourself** and then study yourself some more, then you can know who you truly are. You may ask why I should study myself; I already know who I am. Do you know yourself? Then answer this simple question, are you controlled by your conscious or subconscious thoughts? Who is controlling your thinking, is it your conscious or subconscious? If you are reading this and you are not reading this aloud, then who is talking, and who is listening? Your mouth is not moving, but you hear it, and it is not your ears doing the hearing. I suggest you go and study yourself and learn the mystery of you.

46.   **Never be afraid** of your goals. Just go for it and do not look back until you reach it. Plan your future and plan your days or someone will

plan it for you. Always be thinking ahead. Life is like playing chess, think before you move!

47.   **Stay ahead of your goals** and you will always be ahead of the game called "Life." Decide what you are going to do and just do it. See it and believe it. Read your goals in the morning and at night. Keep your eyes on your goals and do not waste your time on other people's goals, unless it will help you reach yours faster.

48.   **Mind your own business**. Whatever you want to do, just do it. Start small and watch it grow. Do something that you love to do, and you will never work a day in your life. Have you ever seen someone start a small business and years later became a bigger business? Work for yourself part-time for full pay, and have a plan written on paper. Take the time to foretell your future, not someone else's. Now you are minding your own business. Remember to have a successful business doing something you love to do, not just something you like to do.

49.   **We are like walking batteries** full of energy from birth. As we get older, we start to drain our battery, some faster than others.

50.   **If you could not fail** at something, what would you do? If you had all day to do something, what would it be?

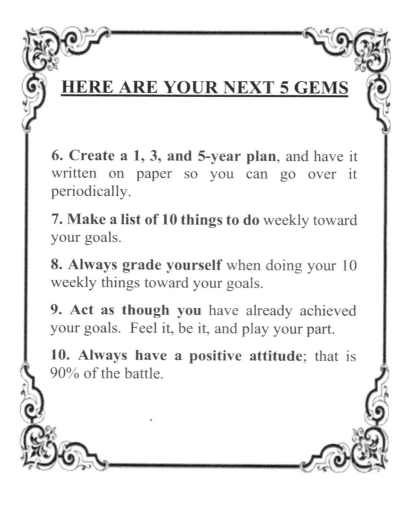

HERE ARE YOUR NEXT 5 GEMS

6. Create a 1, 3, and 5-year plan, and have it written on paper so you can go over it periodically.

7. Make a list of 10 things to do weekly toward your goals.

8. Always grade yourself when doing your 10 weekly things toward your goals.

9. Act as though you have already achieved your goals. Feel it, be it, and play your part.

10. Always have a positive attitude; that is 90% of the battle.

Now that is the closing of Planning Your Future, so heed to the lessons, and reflect on them daily. As I said, this is not a sprint, it is a marathon. Before going on the next steps, write down your 1, 3, and 5-year plan.

Remember if you do not plan to succeed, then you are planning to fail. Make your 10 things to do weekly and grade yourself. This will keep you busy

moving toward your goals to accomplish in five years. Do not forget to act as though you have these things already; like I said, your attitude is 90% of the battle of winning. This next section will touch on your having important goals in life. Did you know some people do not have any real goals, they work, sleep, eat, and take a trip every now and then? I am not saying anything bad about that. Imagine if the Creator said you can have anything you want, do you think that would be it? Of course not, that is what this next section is all about.

Your Goals

This is one of the most important Gems in this book. Let me take you on two journeys, one person with goals and the other without. Let us start off with the one with no goals. Their life goes like this: They wake up on a Monday wishing it were Friday. They do not like their job and wish that the day goes by fast, so they can go home and watch TV and play on their Phone. Did you know that 85 % of the people that work do not like their job? They are just going through the routine just to pay the bills, and they do it for 40 years with just enough to get by at the age of 65 if they are lucky. 40 years just working for someone else to give them a pension if they are lucky again. Now let us take the one with goals. Each morning this person is figuring out how do I get out of this rat race; even if I win, I am still a rat. This person set goals and works toward them day in and day out until they can start their own business. This is more exciting than just going to work and waiting for 40 years to retire. I would take door number 2 all day; this way I am excited for 40 years and maybe a multi-millionaire. You see, I cannot be a millionaire working for some company. Let me retract that. There are a few people with high-level positions that retires amazingly comfortable. Those people are no more than 5 % of the population and even less than that.

51.   **Get excited daily about your goals**. Why, you must get excited about your goals because no one else will. You must speak it into existence, and you must be exciting day in and day out every day, as though you have achieved your goal. It must resonate in your speech and in your manners and you must act as it is so.

52.   **Why listen to motivational speakers**? They will give you energy and insightfulness, to see beyond your own reasoning. They are the coaches that we never had to push us closer to success.

53.   **Stay off your phone** and TV. Why, when you spend time on your phone watching Tik Tok, or on Facebook for hours getting likes, you are paying with your time. Time is valuable and the time you spent may not

get you closer to your goals. You waste an hour here and an hour there when you could be moving an hour closer to your goals.

54. **You should be excited** about working toward your goals in life. Imagine having 10 goals and accomplishing all of them in 3 years. Can you imagine how that will feel? You may add 10 more goals and accomplish that as well. The point here is to have goals that you are excited about that moves you toward your future. Be excited about your goals and finish them and never look back.

55. **Vision is more powerful** than knowledge. If you have a vision, you can do anything. Everything around you have been created with a vision first.

56. **There is a wise saying**, Man who chases after 2 birds captures none. The meaning is to focus on one thing at a time. Regarding goals, focus on one goal at a time. You can have many goals you want to work on but work on one at a time and finish them. You will get a good feeling of joy and accomplishment.

57. **If it does not feel right**, do not do it, when going through the motions with your goals. You should be excited, and it should feel good.

At any point it does not feel right, you need to analyze it very carefully and probably not do it. At this point, you might want to get some advice from a good reliable source, someone that can help you make a good sound decision.

58.   **Stop wasting time** on your phone if you are working on a project, like your goals. You should put away your phone and check it after you have done some of your 10 tasks for the week.

59.   **Act immediately** if it is something that you want to do, and it is positive. Apply the **2-minute rule**. If it only takes **2 minutes** just do it without thinking about it. This applies to your goals in life and many other things that are on your to-do list.

60.   **The Law of attraction** is especially important to completing goals in life. You must pretend that you have already completed that goal. You must act, talk, and walk as though you have these things. Capture the feeling and the emotion that this is what I have done, and you did an excellent job at it and people are thanking you every day for such a great accomplishment.

61.   **We all vibrate** on different frequencies. You must get together with people that will uplift you and help you accomplish your goal faster. This is important, everyone works better with a support team.

62.   **Everything happens for a reason**. This is true, especially when you understand "**The Law of Attraction."** What you think about you bring about. You will be attracting people and things to come your way.

63.   **Remember to be** honest with yourself and others. Make big goals not small ones and you will feel much better when you achieve them. Your goals should be realistic, not something impossible.

64.   **Stay focused**. Staying focused is the key to success.

65.   **Go with your gut feeling**. We all have a sense of inner feeling when something is right or wrong. Follow that feeling and do what is right.

66.   **Always think** of the big picture. Go for what you want in life. Life is too short to let things pass you by; you may never get a second chance.

67.   **The world is changing** every second, so do not be surprised. There are thousands of tools on your computer and phone that you can use

to create things, so use them to your advantage. You will be surprised if you just ask a question: How can I do this or that? Remember you are a creator so create.

68.   **Learn as much as you can**. It only takes 5 years to be an expert in a subject. Study your craft and be one of the best of the best and collaborate with the best and see what comes out of it. Teamwork makes the dream work.

69.   **Work smarter** every day for yourself. Remember you work 40 hours for someone else, so you should spend at least 10 hours a week working for yourself. Do not waste time watching tv stars, which will not help you advance in your life.

70.   **Make each day count** towards your goals.

71.   **Invest in yourself** and make it something you love to do.

72.   **If you do not** put a timer on it, you may lose track of it.

73.   **Never doubt** the power of belief. You must believe that you can do something for you to achieve it, then work toward it.

74. **Stay focused** and learn from past mistakes. Mistakes are the only ways that did not work. They are there to learn from, and to make you smarter and wiser.

75. **Stay calm** and move forward. Plan your way to success. Take your time and make it happen.

76. **Always stay positive**, no matter what the outcome is.

77. **Tomorrow is a mystery**, and today is that mystery. What you do today will be the results of your tomorrow, so make today count.

78. **Toxic people** are all around you, stay away from them. You are the result of your successes and failures and remember you can only control what you do, and not others.

79. **Your 5 closes friends** are the sum of your wealth. So, pick successful wealthy friends and you will become wealthy in time.

80. **Never be afraid** of change. The world is changing every second so you must be prepared to change when the time comes, for you to move forward faster.

81.   **The world is always talking** to you; you just need to know how to listen to it. Listen and observe.

82.   **Never feel guilty** for any minor mistakes that you make, just keep on trying until you get it right.

83.   **Every day is** a brand-new beginning. So, treat it that way, and move closer to your goals.

84.   **Learn all you can,** so you can do all you can. Remember that knowledge is power, and a lack of knowledge is a lack of power.

<u>HERE ARE YOUR NEXT 3 GEMS</u>

11. Get excited daily about your goals.

12. Always listen to motivational speakers that can uplift you to do better in life.

13. Stop · wasting time playing on your phone and watching tv. Now, you have a blueprint for creating your goals. Remember them by revisiting them daily until you have them·memorized. this is the foundation of a successful life, having important goals to live for. Are you ready for the next section? This is one of my favorite sections. It is called "**The Book óf Wisdom**".

Are you ready for the next section?

This is one of my favorite sections, it is called,

"The Book of Wisdom."

The Book of Wisdom

The book of wisdom is all about making you a wise and prudent thinker, meaning you learn from other people's actions, and you think before you act. We travel in life never knowing what lies ahead of us. But we all have an inner awareness of right and wrong. Let us adventure down that mysterious path.

85.   **Pay attention** to your surroundings! Here is an important message: when you feel the spirit telling you to do something, just be brave and do it. **SOURCE (GOD)** brings people together for a reason. Let me give you a quick example. Let us say I am in the park walking, and I overhear someone talking about the pains they have in their legs, and I feel the spirit telling me to tell that person about **Grounding**. I should just go and introduce myself and tell them about the **Grounding**

Method, which they can do for free. Now that person can get some relief immediately when they ground themselves that day. Now, do you see how **SOURCE** works through people? And that is a true story!

86.   **Pay attention when you are driving**. Remember that a few seconds can cost you your life and or thousands of dollars. Some accidents cannot be replaced with money, like the loss of a loved one. Texting on the phone can kill you and others, so please do not text while driving. You do not have to answer all phone calls. And remember that most phone calls are asking for either your time or money. Did you know that wearing your seat belt increases your survival rate by 75 %, I like those odds. That is why, I always wear my seat belt.

87.   **Do not rush things**. Rushing makes for mistakes. Life is full of wonderful things to see and do. When you are young you wish to be older and when you are older you wish to be younger. So do not rush time, because you cannot, and just know that time will come.

88.   **Do not let anyone rush you** when you are driving. Be patient with everything you do. Do not let people rush you to do anything; you may regret it for the rest of your life.

89.   **Your environment** is what dictates your behavior. So, pick your environment very carefully. It will be part of your future.

90.   **Stroll and observe** your surroundings. Take frequent walks in the park and observe nature, including the birds, trees, flowers, and the sky up above. Study nature to understand yourself.

91.   **The Creator has created** all things with a purpose. Now reflect on your life and find your true purpose. You will feel it in your heart and soul that this is it when you find it. Here is the secret, it is always with you.

92.   **Remember, there are no two trees** that are identical, just like there are no two people that are the same. Never forget that God made different flowers. People are like flowers; they are all different in their own ways.

93.   **Keep your eyes and ears open** and see what others are saying and doing around you. These things are also messages for you to hear and see. Do you know what you are hearing and seeing means? It is up to you to figure it out. It could be something or maybe not. Just remember what you

are hearing during the day. It may connect with something later during the day, or another time soon. Just keep that thought in your mind.

94.   **Try to have an original thought** sometime. Do not mimic things you heard if you have not done the research yourself. Always try to think ahead. Life is like playing chess, think before you move. What should you be thinking of at this moment in your life? List 10 important things to do and what is your next move in accomplishing these things. List 10 things to do this week, and just do them. You will feel happy at the end, trust me when I tell you.

1.	6.
2.	7.
3.	8.
4.	9.
5.	10

95.   **Think before you speak**. Your words can cause wars and hurt people. Be a prudent thinker, which means you think before you act. Remember that what you say and do around others will and can affect the way they act and think around you. Do not let alcohol talk you into trouble. Words are powerful. They cut deeper than a knife.

96.   **Know when to speak** and when to be silent. Talking out of turn can get you in trouble and talking out of anger can start fights. Like I said some passage ago be a prudent thinker; that is, act on thought rather than impulse.

97.   **Remove all bad taste** from your mind and your mouth because it is not healthy for the body, or the soul. Life is too short to waste it on ill feelings; snap out of it and move on with your life. Do not hold bad feelings in your heart, it only hurts you and not the other person. Enjoy the present, and the gift called life. Do not forget thousands of people are dying daily; so, do not rush yourself to an early grave.

98.   **Never hate.** Always love. It is healthier to smile than to frown. Life is full of options; you can turn left, or you can turn right, you can act happy, or you can act sad. Remember to spread love everywhere you go.

You can hate the rain or love it. Remember, rain makes beautiful rainbows and provides food.

99.   **Whatever is out of sight** is out of mind. Never put something away that you want to remember. If you do, make a note to remind yourself of those things. Always have it in sight, only if you want to remember it daily. It is extremely easy to forget something if you do not make a note of it to remind you.

100.   **Always take your time** when making any decisions, big or small. Ask yourself if you need it and how is this beneficial to your life. Is this going to help me or harm me in the future? You should always ask yourself these questions when making any decision.

101.   **Remember, it is easier to keep up**, rather than trying to catch up. This is where time plays an especially important part in your life. What you do today will affect your tomorrow, and you do not have all the time in the world. Remember today is just a result of your yesterday's. You get out what you put in.

102.   **Do not be foolish**, stupid, or a dunce! Just think first and seek wisdom. We all have a check system in our minds and body that lets us

know if we are doing something right. Please use your insight and obey it. One mistake can cause many years of pain and suffering. You owe it to yourself to use this book to your advantage.

103.   **Who likes a crybaby** or a person that whines about how bad it is! These are all life lessons to grow from; they will make you stronger if you do not quit. Remember we need to have some tough times to appreciate the enjoyable time ahead.

104.   **Remember to stay calm**. Never let them see you sweat. Do not panic; think first, then act. Just pray and **Source** will direct you if you learn to listen to the message around you. Do not forget, you are never alone. Remember that everything happens for a reason, it is called cause and effect.

105.   **Read books** that are good for the soul and mind. Remember to study yourself and listen to **Sadhguru – Inner Engineering.**

106.   **I ask myself** do I have a soul? I have a soul that lives forever. My soul is living in my body, having a physical experience, and my soul can never die. Spirits are real, and so are our souls.

107.   **Always be strong** and voice your opinion but remember for every action there is a reaction. You will get out of life what you put into your life.

108.   **Be honest.** Do not try to cheat anyone, because it will come back at you and haunt you in the future. Be honest so you do not have to keep looking over your shoulder. It is hard to move forward when you are looking backward.

109.   **Listen to others.** Remember: you do not have to act, just listen. The homeless have a story to tell, the drug addict has an especially important story to tell, and your parents, family, and friends all have a story to tell. Everyone has a message, some good news, and some sad news, but it is just news to learn from.

110.   **Follow your inner instincts.** That is your guide to your future. This is a part of you that most people do not understand. Try not to second-guess these inner thoughts and just do it (only applies to good thoughts). Your inner spirit will know, long before your mind has time to think. So, follow your inner spirit and it is always talking to you, long before you have a chance to answer.

111.   **Treasure your friends**. Friends are one of the only important things that have real value. Some people pretend to be your friend. This is how you can tell a true Friend. Loyal friends do not always ask for something will they call you.

112.   **Do not feel sad** about making a mistake. Just learn from it and do not make the same mistake twice. We must make mistakes in life to learn. Learn from your mistakes, or you will repeat them later.

113.   **Wisdom is learn** not given. Wisdom comes from learning from other people's mistakes. This book is all about learning from people and your experiences in life. Some mistakes can cost you a fortune, while others can cost you your life. Please take heed of the many lessons in this book and learn from them, and you will stand a better chance of understanding your life. Use this book to keep track of all your mistakes and accomplishments and teach these lessons to others.

114.   **Remember the good times** in your life and forget about the tough times. Remember, heaven and hell are within you. Plan to have a good life and create a vision board to remind you of your future. See the future and strive to achieve it, see it, and believe it, and work toward it. Do not

forget you are the controller of your destiny. What you do today will affect your future for tomorrow. Understand that the media (TV) is only programming you to think a certain way.

115.   **There will always be** lesser and greater people than yourself. Everyone deserves respect so respect them all. You do not know what put them in that situation. They too have a lesson to share with you; if you can ask them what put them in that situation, they may tell you and you can learn from their mistakes or mishaps. Life is full of life lessons; learn as you travel through it.

116.   **Be thankful** for the things you have, and do not have in your life. Thank God for the present that you are free and remember this is your gift from the Gods.

117.   **Remember** the homeless person you saw, remember the passing of a loved one, and remember your life could be worse, so appreciate the things you have and do not have. If there is something in life that you want, just plan a way to get it and go for it.

118.   **Try to find** the good in people. If you can bring out the best quality in people, it will help them with self-development. Sometimes all

50

a person needs are a good word of encouragement to bring out the best in them. We all need love in our life. Just hearing that you are doing an excellent job, is what some of us need to hear to advance us to the next hurdle. Find true love and hold on to it with your life.

119.   **Thank God** for every day and every evening because this is your present from GOD today. If you think you have it bad, just hear someone else's problem and you will realize that your problem is not that bad. Remember there will always be lesser and greater people all around you, so do not feel bad about your present situation, just do something about it.

120.   **Do not panic**. Think first, then act. Most things are not as bad as they appear. Failure is good if you get up and try again.

121.   **Most things can be** repaired, just give it a minute or two and think of a solution. After careful thought, you will realize that it was not particularly bad in the first place. Take, for example, the last mistake you made; you got out of it and now you realize that it was not worth all the worry you thought it was. So, anything short of murder, do not panic.

122.   **Always think positively** no matter the situation. You will attract positive things toward you. Always have a positive outlook on life and the world will remember you that way, as the one who saw the good in everything.

123.   **Think positive** and life will be full of joy.

124.   **Be happy** where you are in life. Be the change you want to see in the world and change will come in time.

125.   **Never be jealous** of someone or something. Jealousy is a disease. Let it go.

126.   **Do not be afraid**. Be brave, and realize it was not bad after all.

127.   **Do not let** others rent space in your head. Remember, those who you think about the most control you. Let it go and move on with your life. You do not have time to think about other people and what they may or may not be saying about you.

128.   **Be a person with integrity** and never change your ways.

129.   **If you want to be** a star, hang around stars. If you want to be a fool, hang around fools. Do not watch the news every day, because it will present negative images and thoughts in your mind every day.

130.   **You need people** and people need you. Do not be afraid to ask for help when you need it and give it when the time arrive.

131.   **Use what God has given you.** God has given us all a special gift, find it and use it. Know that you are a child of God. Believe nothing and question everything.

132.   **You will make** plenty of mistakes if you are trying to accomplish things in life and that is okay. Fall 8 times and get up 9 times. Learning from your mistakes is smart. Learning from others' mistakes makes you wise.

133.   **One life**, one love, one purpose with many goals. Have your own personal library at home. Books that inspire learning. A delightful book is like a great meal. Sometimes you just cannot get enough of it.

134.   **Wisdom comes** to those who master ignorance. No man is free until he has mastered himself.

135.   **We are not here** for ourselves; we are here for others. Getting help is good! Being able to help others is better!

136.   **The universe** will guide you, just follow it. Look, listen, and obey. If you want to make God laugh, tell him what you are planning.

137.   **Do not** pre-judge people. That is a big mistake on your part. You never know what someone is all about. Let them show you who they are through their actions and words.

138.   **Do not tell anyone** your secrets, only if you do not want it to remain a secret.

139.   **There is a time** to think and a time to act. Think before you act.

140.   **What you think** may not always be true. Nobody is right all the time, including you.

141.   **There is a real reason** and a good reason. Act on the real reason. Teach as many people as possible. Do not have faith, know the facts. You want to learn something new every day.

142.   **When working on** a project it will behoove you to find a partner that is skilled in that subject of business and is also successful in that field. Your success starts with you and should involve others. Your thoughts are the keys that matters if you want to unlock your goals. You can work faster working together, and no one person can make it on their own.

143.   **Do not have a partner** with a bad reputation and/or is a failure in their actions.

144.   **Never trust** one book to tell you the whole truth, read many books.

145.   **Learn how to** play the game of life but learn the rules first. If you want to win the game, learn how to win. Study winners and losers.

146.   **Your life is** only so many days long, so take full advantage of it every day.

147.   **Your Time** is short. You only have on average: 76 winters, 76 summers, 76 springs, and 76 falls. So, what are you going to do with your time?

148.   **Learn the rules** of the game of life that you are playing. Every game has rules said and unsaid. Play to win but be as fair as possible.

149.   **Your mind** is like a universe full of creations. So, create whatever your mind desires through your thoughts. United Negro College Fund said, "A mind is a terrible thing to waste." So, why don't you use it before you lose it? Have you notice some people have already lost their minds, think about it.

150.   **Learn to build** wealth and good health and remember that wisdom is more precious than gold or silver.

151.   **Treasure the minutes** and the hours because the next minute or hour is not promise to you. Practice Memento Mori, which is remembering death.

152.   **If God** gives you something or someone, treasure it for life.

153.   **Do not judge** anyone. You do not know yourself. How can you judge others?

154.   **Do not spend** hours watching TV unless you are learning something. Try not to waste time. It is all that you have on this planet, in the end.

155.   **If you live** an unjust life, you will always have to look back never knowing what is in front of you.

156.   **Always be polite** to others because you want people to be polite to you.

157.   **Mimic me not** but understand me so.

158.   **If two people tell** you something, pay attention. If three people tell you something, just do it (only if it helps you). It should help you to listen to your friends when they say to bring a coat or umbrella with you, so just bring it. It may seem useless at the time, but believe me, you will wish you had it.

159.   **Knowing life secrets**. It is all about controlling and understanding the inner you. **(Study Sadhguru-Inner Engineering)**

160.   **You cannot push someone** to believe what you believe. Just lead by example and they will see the good in what you believe.

161.   **Know your good** and unhealthy habits. Lack of Growth will diminish you. Remember the way you do something is the way you do all things.

162.   **Always put things** you need in front of the things you want. If you prioritize the things, you want over the things you need, then your needs will be neglect, and you may be unable to achieve your goals.

163.   **Remember when you start** doing something that seems difficult, you will find it to be easier as you keep doing it. See it, believe it, and achieve it.

164.   **Put your life in order** of importance. God first, family second and you third. Remember we are here for others.

165.   **Life is beautiful** if you think it is. Life is hell if you think it is. It is up to you. What do you think about your life?

166.   **Is your glass half empty** or half full? Both answers are correct. It is what you believe. Always believe that things are possible. If they can send a man to the moon, you can achieve about any earthly goal.

167.   **Everyone gets a chance** in life. Will you be ready when it comes your way? It is here now!

168.   **Love your family** and they will love you. Respect your friends, and they should respect you.

169.   **All loss is** the result of a scattering consciousness. Stay focused and stay on your course—not somebody else's. Follow your dreams. Get help when you need it or when others say that you need it. Do you understand, young ones? Believe in your dreams and get advice from those who already accomplished your dreams. Whatever you want to do or be in life, be it, and do it. Just know you can always find a way.

170.   **Always take your time** when making any decisions, big or small. Remember GOD does not make failures, people do.

171.   **Study the Gods** and Goddesses of the world from Egypt, India, China, Greece and Rome, and all others, which shows wisdom and intellect. Knowledge is particularly good to taste, and you will not get full of it! Remember, all I know is all I know. What I learned in my many years is that I know nothing

172. **Understand that you have power** far beyond your understanding. Learn to tap into your inner powers.

173.   **Death is real,** and so are you!

174. **"It is not that I am afraid** to die, I just do not want to be there when it happens," Woody Allen.

175. **"No one is going** to give you the education you need to overthrow them. Nobody is going to teach you your true history, teach you your true heroes, if they know that that knowledge will help set you free."
— **Assata Shakur**

176. **I leave you with** these words, only to help guide you through life. The teacher will stop teaching when the student stops listening.

177. **Pay attention** to your dreams, it will tell you who you really are and expose some of the deepest thoughts that are in your subconscious mind. Ask yourself these questions. How old are you in your dreams? Can you tell yourself one color you saw in your dreams? Did you really see a face in your dreams? Try to think in your dreams, that you are dreaming. Only then will you start to take control of the dream that you are having. Why are their no mirrors in your dreams.

178. **Study your God**, read about other Gods, and remember, your God should look like you, not like your oppressor.

179. **Every day is** a good day. If you do not think so, try missing one. The catch is you cannot just miss just one day.

180. **You are never** too old or too young to learn. Knowledge is ageless, and wisdom is for everyone, learn from your own mistakes and achievements and learn from others.

181. **Follow** *Billy Carson*, **_Bruce Lipton_**, *Sadhguru*, **_Jordan Peterson_**, *19 Keys*, **_Dr. Sebi_**, *Professor Smalls*, **_Phil Valentine_**, *blackmagik363, and* **_Yahki Awakened_**.

182. **People vibrate** on all different frequencies. Did you ever meet someone for the very first time and had a bad vibe about that person? You both are on two different frequencies; likewise, have you ever met someone for the very first time and you both just hit it off and were attach to each other? It does not have to be a sexual vibe, just a harmonist feeling about each other.

183. **The teacher will appear** only when the student is ready. Study **"The Kybalion"** and the **7 Hermetic principles**, and you will get clarity about the world around you.

184. **Your words have power** over others if they let it. Never let anyone disturb your peace.

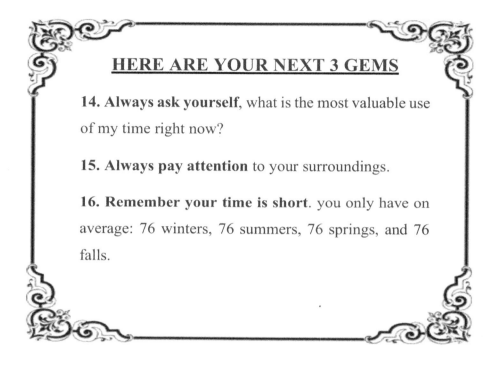

HERE ARE YOUR NEXT 3 GEMS

14. Always ask yourself, what is the most valuable use of my time right now?

15. Always pay attention to your surroundings.

16. Remember your time is short. you only have on average: 76 winters, 76 summers, 76 springs, and 76 falls.

Now, how did you like the Book of Wisdom, it is one of my favorites. I listen to it all the time, so I will not forget some of the important lessons in this book. Now that you heard some important lessons in the Book of Wisdom, it is time to talk about some good and unhealthy habits.

Good and Unhealthy Health Habits

Before we start, I must make this disclaimer, I am not a doctor, and this is for informational purposes only. If you need medical help, see your doctor. We all know what good health habits are, we just tend to ignore them until it becomes a major problem, such as we should not be using drugs of any kind because they can be addictive. Now we really have a problem when all we think of is that drug. Imagine doing that for 5 years straight. That is insane and now you are no longer in control of your body and mind. You are now in the hand of substance abuse, and you need to get help from an outsider to bring your lost soul back to yourself. You have lost control—now do not travel down that lonely dark road.

185. **Ask yourself** this simple, but not so simple question: What is the most important thing in your life? It should only be one answer, and that

is your health. Without your health, you will be struggling to survive. Keep in mind most diseases can be reverse. Check out Yahki-Awakened, he has cured thousands of people, with natural foods and herbs. Check out the young Master of Health and wellness. Now it is up to you, what are you going to do?

186. **Exercise daily**. Why, your body is like a machine. What happens when you let your car just sit parked for many years? The parts get rusted, the seal gets brittle and cracked and the engine may seize up on you. You need to move and exercise your body, so they become flexible and pliable, meaning able to bend and twist in many directions. There is a saying, use it or lose it. The same is true for your body parts. Exercise is one of the keys to being healthy in your life.

187. **Ground yourself**. Why, this is especially important to ground yourself. It will get rid of some inflammation in your body that is causing you pain, and illnesses. This is important to having a healthier body and lifestyle. Get the audible book called "**Earthing—The most important health discovery ever" by Clinton Ober**. It will change your life forever. Trust me when I tell you.

188.   **Eat healthily**. Why, this goes with exercise and grounding. Look up **Dr. Sebi** and **Yahki -Awakened** and they will teach you all you need to know about the right foods to put into your body. With all these GMO and seedless fruits, you do not know what you are eating. Studying **Dr. Sebi** and **Yahki Awakened** will change your way of thinking and eating.

189.   **Meditate daily**. Why, this is something that will open your mind and clear your thoughts and will have you tap into your inner self. This will take you away from the outside world and will put you in touch with your inner self, which is the real self. The real you are not the person you see in the mirror. Your soul is the most principal element of who you are. What do God and the Devil both want from you; it is not your body; it is your soul. Why? Because this is the real you. Study **Sadhguru**, you will learn more about yourself.

190.   Substance abuse takes years away from your life and will hurt your body and spirit overall. What you do today will affect you tomorrow. Can you see your future? Good or bad, happy, sad, foolish, or wise. It is up to you and what you do today. Smoking robs your body of oxygen. Many diseases are caused by a lack of oxygen. It is design to get your money and make you addicted to it and one day may seriously harm you.

191.   **Do not drink** cow's milk. Cow's milk is for a cow. Research the other milk to drink, like almond milk. A cow drinks cow's milk. A goat drinks goat's milk. A dog drinks dog milk, and a human drinks his mother's milk. So, what are you putting into your body, pasteurized milk? Pasteurized milk is not good, look it up.

192.   **Do not drink** too much alcohol, soda, or fruit drinks. They have too much sugar and other substances which are not good for your body's growth.

193.   **Stay away from red meat**, white sugar, Dairy, and white flour products. They are also not good for the body. Did you know salt without Iodine can destroy your kidneys? Do you want to keep both of your kidneys in good healthy shape? Watch what you eat. Iodine in salt is good for the body. You can get this in kemp supplement, instead of salt. Eat little to no meat because you are not an animal. Eat things that have a seed in them or grow from seed. That is what God made for you, not hotdogs and hamburgers.

194.   **Know your limit** when eating and drinking. Eating too much can make you unhealthy. Drinking too much can kill you. Eat for tomorrow,

not for today. The delightful Book says to let your food be your medicine and your medicine be your food. Remember you eat for health, not for taste.

195.   **Treasure your body** and brain because it is the only one you have. Learn to juice. Your body absorbs what you breathe, eat and drink. A juicer will extract important nutrients and cleanse the body of toxins.

196.   **Try to heal disease** with natural foods. It is safer and has little to no side effects. Eat plenty of organic foods, foods with seeds in them, and green leafy vegetables. Think healthy. Be wise. Eat healthily and you will live healthier and be full of energy. Remember garbage in, equals garbage out.

197.   **Remember there is only one disease** and that is inflammation— look it up; look up Clinton Ober on earthing. This will blow your mind, it is simple and easy to do, and most of all it is free. It is call **"Grounding."**

198.   **Did you know Dr. Sebi cured cancer?** That is right, I said it, cured cancer! Look him up on YouTube. Buy this book on Amazon: **"Doctor SEBI CURE FOR CANCER**: *How to Treat Cancer with Natural Remedies, Using Dr. Sebi Alkaline Diet Method, and Approach.*

199. Now go to YouTube and **check out Yahki-Awakened**, he also can help you with your health problem using natural foods. As the delightful Book said, "Let your food be your medicine and your medicine be your food."

200. **You need to do** these three things to be healthy: 1. You need to eat Alkaline foods that help nourish the body. **2.** You need to exercise regularly. They say if you do not use it, you will lose it. **3.** You must ground yourself daily.

Now you have it, those are some of "**The Hidden Gems**" to a healthier life. Do not wait until you are sick to think about your health. Health should be the first thing you think about in the morning, afternoon, and evening.

201. **Remember your body** is the vehicle that you travel in, so keep it tuned up. Study your own health for yourself.

202. **Do not take any pills** or vitamins on an empty stomach. If you do you will feel sick. Manufactured medicine is used to suppress the symptoms, not fix the cause.

203.   **Remember to take** two tablespoons of olive oil each day.

204.   **You are your own** friend and foe at the same time.

205.   **Did you know** that Sea Moss contains 90 of the 102 minerals the body needs, if you add **Bladderwrack**, it will take care of all your nutritional needs. Look it up, you will be amazed!

HERE ARE YOUR NEXT 4 GEMS

17. Exercise daily.

18. Ground yourself daily.

19. Know what you are eating, and how it will affect the body. Eat alkaline foods.

20. Meditate daily, do this to focus and contact the real you, which is your soul. This next section is about money. Did you know that most people are working paycheck to paycheck? let us see what we can do about that, in this next section. Called let us talk about Money.

This next section is about money. Did you know that most people are working paycheck to paycheck? let us see what we can do about that, in this next section, called. "**Let us Talk About Money**

Let us Talk About Money

Before I do that, I must make this disclaimer, this is not financial advice. I am not a financial advisor. If you are seeking financial advice, you must seek a financial planner. This is only my experience that I learned in life. Now let us begin.

206.   **Save 10-15%** of the money you earn. Why, having money **tucked away for a rainy day** is wise planning. That is an expression meaning to have saved up money for tough times, and we all will have a challenging time in life. Where we will need extra cash on hand. Savings is exceedingly important to have when there is an emergency in your life. Think about this if you are working then you should be saving some money. You are not working every day, week, month, and year just to pay bills. That would be slavery, working just to pay bills. Where is the

freedom in that? Start saving your money and watch it grow, bigger and bigger by the week, month, and year. Your money should always be working for you and not against you. Save your money and invest it in yourself when you can. Start a small business that makes you passive income. Do not pay full price for designer clothes, shoes, or bags. If you do, you are making the designer richer, while you are getting poorer. Design your own bag, shoes, or clothes to sell. Turn $1,000 into $2,000, into $4,000, into $8,000, into $16,000. Now you have the money to spend as you please. Do not buy an expensive car just to show off, that would not be a sound investment. Now you just added to your expenses, a car that you must work for, or they will take it back. Imagine making enough money to pay cash for the car with no car payments, using the money you made from your business. Think before you start spending your hard earn money and start saving your money to invest in yourself and your family's future.

207.   **Buy a three-family** apartment building when you are young and live in one apartment. **Remember to buy when it is a buyers' market, not when it is a sellers' market**. Why, real estate has always been a great investment, and within about 7 years you should have about $50,000

worth of equity that you can use to buy another investment property with 3 or more units. You are buying assets, not liabilities. Assets bring money in, while liabilities take money from you. It is that simple. Make your first property a multi-unit property and live in one unit. Then a few years later buy your second property. Stay in either property for a few more years and then move out of your first property and rent it out to help pay for a single-family home. Only do this if you see a positive cash flow and it makes financial sense. Do not do this because your friends all have single-family homes. You only do it if the numbers are right.

208. **When buying an investment property** make sure you do your homework. Have someone knowledgeable look it over even if you must pay for their services. Do not decide on your own. If you do that, you could lose thousands of dollars, and it could cause many years of headaches. Be patient. If it is a good deal today, it is a good deal tomorrow.

209. **Keep in mind,** you will never own your own home because you will always have to pay property taxes. So, think about that when you are looking for a home to retire in. When investing, do not rush to invest. Do all your homework and check the numbers twice and remember numbers do not lie. Invest in the future which will someday be the present.

210.	**Do not gamble** at the casinos, horses, or picket machines. These games are design to take your money. Just look at the people around you who gamble, they are trying to win their money back. I say quit when you are ahead, just buying yourself something you would have never bought; you will feel much better later. Do not gamble on something you do not have a real chance of winning. What are the odds? A million to 1, is not good odds. Just take the money and invest it in yourself, you will get a greater return that will last forever.

211.	**Stay out of debt,** except for good debt like buying an investment property, which is generating a positive cash flow. Debt can destroy your marriage, your way of living, and your ability to buy on credit. Poor credit can prevent you from getting a job, an apartment, a loan, and many other things.

212.	**Make good investments**, both big and small and you will be richer in no time. Remember what Warren Buffett said, "Remember **Rule # 1**, do not lose money. **Rule #2**, Do not forget **Rule #1**."

213.	**Invest wisely**. Get help from wise investors, it helps. Invest in something that will bring you continuous money from one sale or idea.

This is how you build true wealth. For example, a book, a song, an invention, an apartment building, etc.

214. **Make four rivers of income** and you will have the freedom that includes free time to spend with your family. Just believe and act toward making it happen.

215. **When spending money,** always think twice. When spending over $100, think three times. When spending over $500, think five times. Ask yourself: Do I really need this? Then, make sure you can return it within 30-90 days (about 3 months). Think of the money you can put away. Just a little bit adds up. Think of the future before you buy something and ask yourself, will it help you today and tomorrow? If the answer is "no," ask yourself if you really need it today.

216. **Keep track of the money** that you are spending, or someone will spend it for you. Check charges on your bank statement, credit cards, and charge cards. And, most of all, put away some savings; like my grandmother said, "You don't know when you will need it." Save 10% of all your earnings for about 5- 10 years and invest it wisely. You should never have to borrow money again for your lifestyle and needs.

217.   **Reconcile your bank statements** once a month because you can have a charge on your account about which you do not know. It happened to me. This went on for 18 months. Not good ($24.95 times 18 months = too much money wasted).

218.   **Cut the fat from your purse** by saving money. 10 things that save money: **1**. Do not pay the designer price, look for sales; **2**. Check your bank statement for errors; **3**. Do not pay a lot for a simple cup of coffee; **4**. Always get a second opinion on auto repair; **5**. Never pay the minimum on your credit card,   always pay off your credit card before the due date. **6**. Shut off the TV if you are not watching it. **7**. Turn off the lights if no one is in that room. **8**. Pack your own lunch. **9**. Skip the drink at the restaurant. Drink water it is free. **10** Create a budget when grocery shopping and shave five dollars on it. Instead of spending $200 per month, make it $195. Try to spend less and save more. Shop at the **Dollar Tree** for savings and check the expiration date. There you have it, **10** ways to save money.

219.   **Never buy a car** by yourself. Always have a skilled mechanic with you before making your purchase. Either pay now or pay later. Buy your dream car and be happy only if you can afford it. Never buy a

salvaged car for full value. Always check online for hidden details about the car that you are purchasing and always, I mean always, have a professional mechanic with you, even if you must pay him. It will be cheaper than trying to return the car. Be careful when buying a used mechanical part for a car. Try to buy new or rebuilt parts with a warranty that have at least a six-month or more warranty coverage. Here is a bonus, cut the cable bill. You are watching the same thing over and over and paying the same amount over and over.

220. **Get a Triple-A gold card**; it is affordable, and it is about $45 if you join with a family member that has a Triple-A gold card. Always check the fluids in your car. Mainly check your antifreeze and your oil, these are the two most important fluid to check regularly. Always keep a can of fix a flat, jumper cable, and Oil and antifreeze in the trunk of your car. This can save you thousands of dollars. Make it a habit to check your oil and antifreeze in your car. If your car ever starts to overheat and get into the red. Stop it immediately and call Triple-A, and have it towed to a mechanic or your home. The Triple-A Gold card will allow you to get toad anywhere up to 100 miles free. Get your Triple-A Gold card, before it is too late, and you may be forced to pay around $100 for service. Now,

that is money you could have saved. Get your Triple-A card today, remember one of your life lessons was not to procrastinate.

221.   **If it looks too good** to be true, 99% of the time it is just that, too good to be true. Do not fall for it. Many people have lost their shirts, believing in a fantasy deal. Do not fall for it, there is a sucker born every day. Remember there is no easy money, you must work for it or get lucky.

222.   **Never buy a brand-new** car. Why? You lose thousands of dollars the day you drive it off the car lot. The same for jewelry.

223.   **Build your credit** score to at least 750 which is consider very good credit score and all things you buy on credit will be cheaper. Build a line of credit to $100,000.00, you never know when a sweet deal will come your way. Do this for your personal line of credit and your business.

224. **You will never see a millionaire** hanging around a homeless person. Two different mindsets. Your Network dictates your Net worth. Never listen to a broke person for financial advice.

225.   **Start saving** at an early age, before 20 years young; this will get you in the habit of being a saver, not a spender. Start saving about 10% to

15% of your earnings for a rainy day; if you cannot then you are not making enough to prosper and you need to fix it.

226. **Think about your retirement** when you are about 21 years young not 60 years old. Do not spend your money like you will always have it. Think about your tomorrow because it is here today.

227. **During questionable times**, be prepared for the worst. That way you will never be off guard. Have an emergency fund, put aside 6-months' worth of living expenses saved, just for tough times. Always have a plan B, but do not use it. Create a budget and stick to it.

228. **Know your trade** outcome. Always have a plan when trading any market. Always have a stop loss when trading options, stocks, or crypto. Invest in what you know. Always have an exit plan when investing and do not forget to secure your profits.

229. **Financial freedom** is what you want for yourself and your family. It is best to work as a team when investing. Take risks but do not be foolish, know what you are doing, and have a stop loss in place. Risk what you are willing to lose without it hurting you or your family's way of living.

HERE ARE YOUR NEXT 2 GEMS

21. Exercise daily. Start saving 10-15% of the money you earn.

22. Ground yourself daily. Buy a three-family apartment building when you are young and live in one of the apartments.

Now let us talk about some good Habits

to have in life.

Good Habits

Good habits build good character. Remember this life is all about the many experiences you have on this planet. You want to have as many good character traits as possible. You want to prove to yourself that you have control over yourself, by being persistent and resistant to the things that do not matter to you. Let us begin learning some good habits.

230. **Do not procrastinate**, just do it. It is easier for you to just do what you are supposed to do in life than to procrastinate the inevitable. It is also easier to keep up rather than to try to catch up. For example, finish high school, then finish College for a bachelor's degree, then go for your master's degree. It should take two years to complete a master's degree, and the rest is on you. Remember time waits for no one.

231.   **Pay attention** when you are driving. Remember that a few seconds can cost you your life and or thousands of dollars. Some accidents cannot be replaced with money, like the loss of a loved one. Texting on the phone can kill you and others so please do not text while driving.

232.   **Always be on time** for school, work, and appointments. It is a good habit to live by; it shows good character, and that you respect other people's time.

233.   **Do not waste your time with negative people.** They will destroy your positive outlook on life. Negative people are only happy when everyone else is unhappy around them. Positive people hang around with other positive people, and negative people hang around with other negative people. I hope you get the picture.

234. **Do not waste time playing games**. Watching senseless TV shows or hanging out when you should be working on your future goals is not a good habit to have. Do not get me wrong, I am not saying do not do these things at all. I am saying to spend 90% of your time taking care of your business, and 10% playing around.

235.   **Keep your eyes** and ears open and see what others are saying and doing around you. Everything around you have a message, but because we are not train in seeing or hearing the messages around us, we miss them. Remember, what you do not know cannot help you.

236.   **Surround yourself** with people that will uplift you. We all need encouragement from one another. Positive people are like premium fuel to a car. It is the best gasoline a car can get; it will perform at a higher performance than regular gas. Positive people do the same to us. They uplift us, support us, and feed our souls with positive energy, so surround yourself with people that will help you grow as a person.

237.   **Be spiritual.** Why, religious people only focus on their belief? They do not want to associate themselves with other religions, not all but some. If you are a spiritual person, then you accept all people and all races of people and religions, because it is not based on your personal affiliation with a group. It is much higher than that, it is your relationship with God under one universal law and that is love for humanity and nature. Be spiritual and love all things around you. Remember you are one with the universe and with God.

238.   **Always think about improving** yourself. Why, why not, do you want to see a better version of yourself each day, week, and year? You will upgrade your phone, car, and electronic devices, but you will not upgrade yourself. If that is the case, then you might have your priorities out of order. Improve yourself by strengthening your weaknesses and you will live a better and happier life. Let us see what the 3.0 version of you looks like.

239.   **Start feeding your soul**. Why, this is important also. Most people do not know what to feed the soul. Most people do not know or believe they have a soul. Your soul and spirit are the same. You need knowledge of your soul, and you need to be reminded of yourself that you are not the body and that your soul is having a bodily experience. I hope I did not lose you by saying that. Imagine a snail in a shell, that shell is not the snail. The shell is the housing of the snail, just like your body is the housing of your soul. Do you follow me? Now you must feed the soul knowledge of itself, so you the doer in the body can have a better understanding of who you really are.

240. **You should always be asking** yourself, what is the most valuable use of my time, right now?

241.   **Belief is half the battle** in doing anything. To start or break a habit, do, or do not do something for 21 days. Positive thinking is the key to success, followed by action.

242.   **Learn the basics** of any and everything you try to do. Learning is the ability to understand something. Learn how to make money, study, cook, fight, and meditate, love and how to be a better you.

243. **Try not to lie** to your children, because they will lie to you; they are only a reflection of you.

244. **Listen and learn.** We all have stories to tell. Write them down and pass them on to your family to learn from. Write down the things that make you happy, and do more of them, only if they are positive and are heading toward your future.

245. **When spending your money**, always expect the best in return; get in the habit of investigating your purchases. (Do some research; do not be an impulsive shopper, you will lose a lot of money that you could be saving). Remember it is not how much money you make; it is how much money you save.

246. **Read books** that are good for the soul and mind and that inspire you to want more out of life. Remember to study yourself and your behavior; why? Because you want to know yourself better.

247. **It is good** to discipline a child when they are young and not let them talk back to you as though you are the child. You can lose control amazingly fast, and you do not want that to happen. Your child will soon be an adult, and what do you think will happen if they do not listen to you? Do you think they will listen to their teacher? Of course not, this is because you let them get out of control. This is not good for either one of you, so correct it before it gets out of hand.

248. **Never call your child** stupid, dumb, or crazy. In psychology, the first 7 years of child development will program the child's behavior. It has been well proven that you can steer a child in any direction that you choose at an early age. In knowing that, I call my child a superstar all her life. She has exceeded my expectations; in things, I could not have imagined. She now attends a prestigious college to acquire a Doctorate degree and a PhD. She will become a doctor and a scientist, and the first 7 years help mold her to strive for greatness as a superstar. If you keep calling your child stupid, do not be surprised if your programming works.

249."**To lead people,** walk beside them. . . As for the best leaders, the people do not notice their existence. The next best, the people's honor and praise. The next, the people fear; and the next, the people hate. . . When the best leader's work is done the people say, we did it ourselves — Lao Tzu

250. Never wish to be someone else. Just be the best you can be. Study your weaknesses and master your strengths. Remember tomorrow is a new day to begin something new or to continue focusing on your goals. If you are weak in a subject, strengthen it with a little practice each day. See into your future by planning your days. Never say I cannot because you can if you try long enough.

251.   **When talking** to your friends and family be firm and honest. If they are doing something good let them know it, and if they are doing something bad let them know that.

252.   **Do not put all your eggs** in one basket. If the basket breaks, so do all your eggs. This applies to everything in your life. When investing, do not bet the farm on one thing. When gambling, do not spend or bet all

your money. When dealing with people do not put all your faith in any person, because they might let you down.

253. **Remember the lessons** that are in this book, it will save you time, money, and grief. Trust me when I tell you this.

254. **Learn how to swim**, it may save your life and others' as well. There is a Chinese saying that goes like this. The best time to plant a tree was 20 years ago. The next best time is now. So, learn how to swim now.

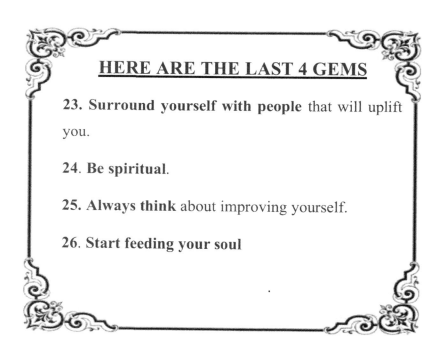

HERE ARE THE LAST 4 GEMS

23. Surround yourself with people that will uplift you.

24. Be spiritual.

25. Always think about improving yourself.

26. Start feeding your soul

Let us recap "**The 26 Hidden Gems**".

26 Hidden Gems

1.   **Take an aptitude test** or job placement test. Why, because it will save you time, money, and headaches, and it will point you in the right direction at an early age.

2.   **Finish high school**, or college or get certified in many things. Why, in this book I talk about how it is easier to keep up rather than trying to catch up. In high school, you should be with people that are going to college or have goals of starting their own business.

3.   **Watch "The Secret."** Why, this is one of the foundations to becoming successful in life. You must

believe in yourself before you can believe in others. "**The Secret**" is all about "**The Laws of Attraction**."

4.   **Create a vision board.** Why, you need a vision board to see where you want to go in life, and you need to see the things you want to accomplish.

5.   **Have a list of 25 things to accomplish** in the next 5 years. Why, your life should always be about accomplishing things. If you do not do these things, you are wasting your time doing senseless things that do not amount to anything in your life in the end.

6.   **Have a 1, 3, and 5-year plan.** Why, if you do not plan your life someone will plan it for you.

7.   **Have a list of 10 things** to do per week. Make a list of 10 things to do every week that will bring you closer to accomplishing the things on your list of 25 things to accomplish.

8.   **Grade yourself** in doing your 10 weekly things toward your goals. The things that you have on your list you must take very seriously and do not play with this; these are your future and your goals to accomplish in

the next five years. 5 Years will come, will you be on your time or someone else's time. It is up to you, and it starts now.

9.   **Act as though you have** it already.   Why, this is also important you must walk, talk and function as though you have all these things on your list, and this is where **"The Law of Attraction"** come in. As you travel through life the universe will bring these things toward you. You must be ready to capture it and recognize it when it comes.

10.   **Always think positively**. Your attitude is a big part of getting what you want in life. You must always think positively in life and not negatively.

11.   **Get excited daily** about your goals. Why, you must get excited about your goals because no one else will.

12.   **Listen to motivational speakers**. They will give you an insight into life and motivate you in ways you could not imagine.

13.   **Always ask yourself,** what is the most valuable use of my time right now? You want to always be asking yourself what you should be doing right about now that will bring you closer to your goals in life.

14. **Stay off your phone** and TV. When you spend time on your phone watching Tik Tok, or on Facebook for hours getting likes, you are paying with your time. Time is valuable and the time you spent may not get you closer to your goals

15. **Pay attention to your surroundings**. Why, if you are talking to the **SOURCE(GOD)**, the **SOURCE** will respond in many unimaginable ways. You just need to pay attention to your surroundings. Every voice you hear, every action you see, every feeling you should be paying attention to it.

16. **Save 10-15%** of the money you earn. Savings are exceedingly important to have when there is an emergency in your life, or when a great investment comes your way.

17. **Buy a three-family apartment** building when you are young and live in one apartment. Real estate has always been a great investment, and within about 7 years you should have about $50,000 worth of equity that you can use to buy another 3-family property. Only buy when it is a buyers' market.

18.   **Exercise daily.** It is a healthy thing to do, to keep your body in good working condition.

19.   **Ground yourself.** It will help get rid of some inflammation in your body and that is particularly important to have a healthy body and lifestyle.

20.   **Eat alkaline food**. You are what you eat. You should be eating only alkaline foods, this will nourish the body, and keep disease away.

21.   **Meditate daily**. Why, this is something that will open your mind and clear your thoughts and will have you tap into your inner self.

22.   **What is the most important thing** to you? It is your health. Why, this should not need an explanation but let me proceed. You have a life, and in this life, you want to create things and live a happier life by doing these things, but without good health, these things you can no longer do.

23.   **Surround yourself with people** that will uplift you. Positive people are like water that will nourish you as a flower. We all need encouragement from one another.

24.   **Be spiritual.** Be spiritual and love all things around you. Remember you are one with the universe and with God.

25.   **Always think** about improving yourself. Do you want to see a better version of yourself each day, week, and year? Let us see what the 3.0 version of you looks like.

26.   **Start feeding your soul.** You must feed the soul knowledge of itself, so you the doer in the body can have a better understanding of who you are.

We have come to the end of this book.

Having listed over 250 life lessons and 26 Gems, we should remember that there is no such thing as an overnight success; it is a fallacy; a myth peddled in a world where someone may have virally capitulated to fame as an internet phenomenon in a matter of 24 hours. But that part, the part we do not see, the part full of failure, learning, and progress, is what makes success possible. What I would like everyone to know in reading this book, "**The Hidden Gems in Life**, "is that it takes work, and there is a process that takes us towards succeeding, in our goals. That process may look like a failure, which only means that we tried but it just did not work.

Focus on improving yourself and being consistent in staying on track. You are not getting it right does not mean you will not. Take note of every point in this book, and it will direct you to success. Failure is unavoidable, it is a part of the many stages toward succeeding. However, this book would help reduce your chances of failing and giving up on your goals. It is amazing how often the time taken to achieve your goals are forgotten; how frequently we forget what lies beyond the tip of an iceberg, the shadowy section under the water.

When you look at the definition of failure in the dictionary, it is defined by three words—lack of success. We do not value growth and learning if we fear failure and imperfections. So, I hope that after reading this book, you have been bold and courageous to make that move toward succeeding, necessary. Take that aptitude test. Get those certificates. Feed your mind. Follow your dreams and fulfill your goals. Watch "**The Secret**" and write down your 25 things to accomplish in the next 5 years. Write 10 things to do weekly towards your goals, and grade yourself and get 12 A's in in a row. Be that champion in your life and prove to yourself that you can do anything that you set your mind to, by applying the many lessons and Gems written in this book. Remember, this book is full of life lessons and

Gems to treasure for the rest of your life to become a better you. I hope you enjoyed this book. I will continue to write and give you more life lessons and Gems to improve your way of living. Until later, that is all, for now. Be Safe and think positive, always. Just keep trying until you succeed. Remember your life, is what you make of it.

References & Citations

You must believe in yourself before you can believe in others. | Keep . . ., https://www. Pinterest. com/pin/you-must-believe-inyourself-before-you-can-believe-in-others-246290673345017585/.

Follow Your Passion and You Will Never Work a Day in Your Life, https://johneengle. com/blog/follow-your-passion/.

If you are the smartest person in the room then you are in the wrong . . ., https://www. homeservicestoronto. com/blog/if-youare-the-smartest-person-in-the-room-then-you-are-in-thewrong-room.

What the Bible says about as he Thinks in his Heart - Bible Tools, https://www. bibletools. org/index. cfm/fuseaction/Topical. show /RTD/cgg/ID/22234/As-he-Thinks-his-Heart. htm.

You Are Not Looking for a Job – Prosperous Physicist, https://www. prosperousphysicist. com/you-are-not-looking-fora-job/.

Be Thankful: 67 Unique Things to Express Gratitude for in Life . . ., https://www. purposefairy. com/98432/things-to-be-thankfulfor/.

There Is a Time to Think and A Time to Act Quotes and Sayings, https://www. searchquotes. com/search/There_Is_A_Time_To_T hink_And_A_Time_To_Act/.

Amy's Words: So, what are You Going to do With Your Time? http://blog. amyswords. com/2016/09/so-what-are-you-goingto-do-with-your_24.html.

Quote by Lao Tzu: "To lead people, walk beside them . . . As for the. . .," https://www. goodreads. com/quotes/10627-to-leadpeople-walk-beside-them-as-for-the.

The Best Time to Plant a Tree - Esri, https://www. esri. com/about/newsroom/arcuser/plant-a-tree/.

Remember you must love yourself before you can truly love someone, http://www. wittyprofiles. com/q/5587364.

You must believe in yourself before you can believe in others. | Keep . . ., https://www. pinterest. com/pin/you-must-believe-inyourself-before-you-can-believe-in-others-246290673345017585/.

Book Pictures are provided by Pixabay and Depositphotos

Image Cover

by Depositphotos

https://depositphotos. com/58434517/stock-photo-book-withmagic-powers. html

Page 1 Image

by Pixabay

https://pixabay. com/illustrations/letter-letter-t-t-initialsfont-2484518/

Page 4 Image

by Pixabay

https://pixabay. com/illustrations/letter-letter-h-h-initialsfont-2484494/

Page- 5 Image

by Pixabay

https://pixabay. com/illustrations/letter-letter-e-e-initialsfont-2484490/

Page 7 Image

by Pixabay

https://pixabay. com/illustrations/letter-letter-h-h-initialsfont-2484494/

Page 9 Image

by Pixabay

https://pixabay. com/illustrations/letter-letter-i-i-initialsfont-2484495/

Page 25 Image

by Pixabay

https://pixabay. com/illustrations/letter-letter-d-d-initialsfont-2484489/

Page 32 Image

by Pixabay

https://pixabay. com/illustrations/letter-letter-d-d-initialsfont-2484489/

Page 41 Image

by Pixabay

https://pixabay. com/illustrations/letter-letter-e-e-initialsfont-2484490/

Page 63 Image

by Pixabay

https://pixabay. com/illustrations/letter-letter-n-n-initialsfont-2484507/

Page 71 Image

by Pixabay

https://pixabay. com/illustrations/letter-letter-g-g-initialsfont-2484492/

Page 81 Image

by Pixabay

https://pixabay. com/illustrations/letter-letter-e-e-initialsfont-2484490/

Page 89 Image

by Pixabay

https://pixabay. com/illustrations/letter-letter-m-m-initialsfont-2484505/

by Pixabay

Page 97 Image

https://pixabay. com/illustrations/letter-letter-s-s-initialsfont-2484517/

Made in the USA
Middletown, DE
15 September 2023

38413479R00056